The N
House

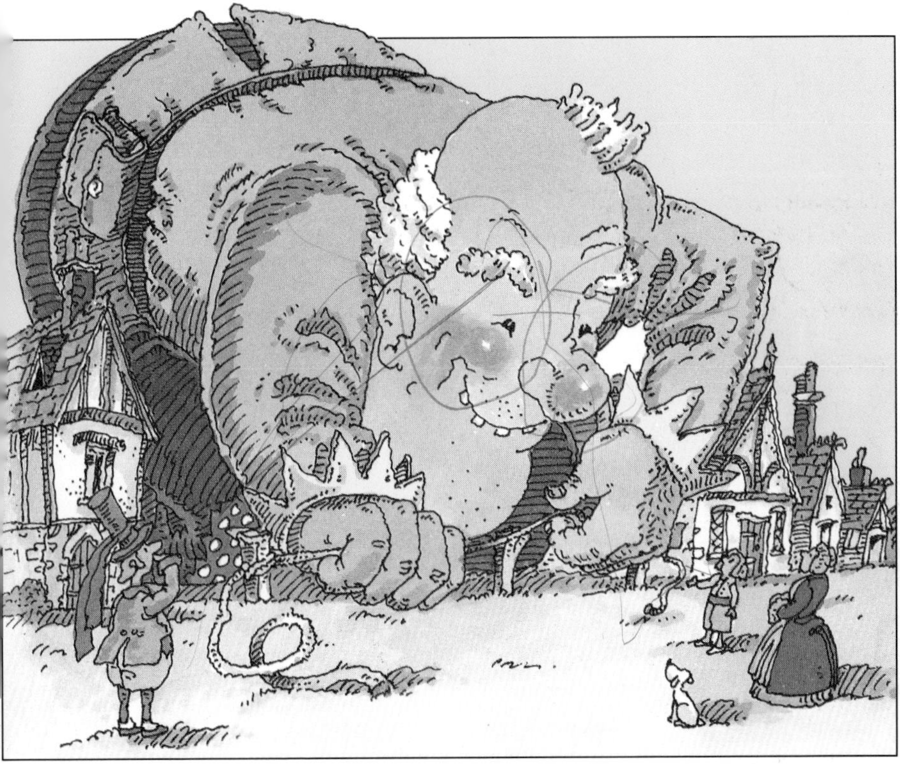

By Ann Wilson

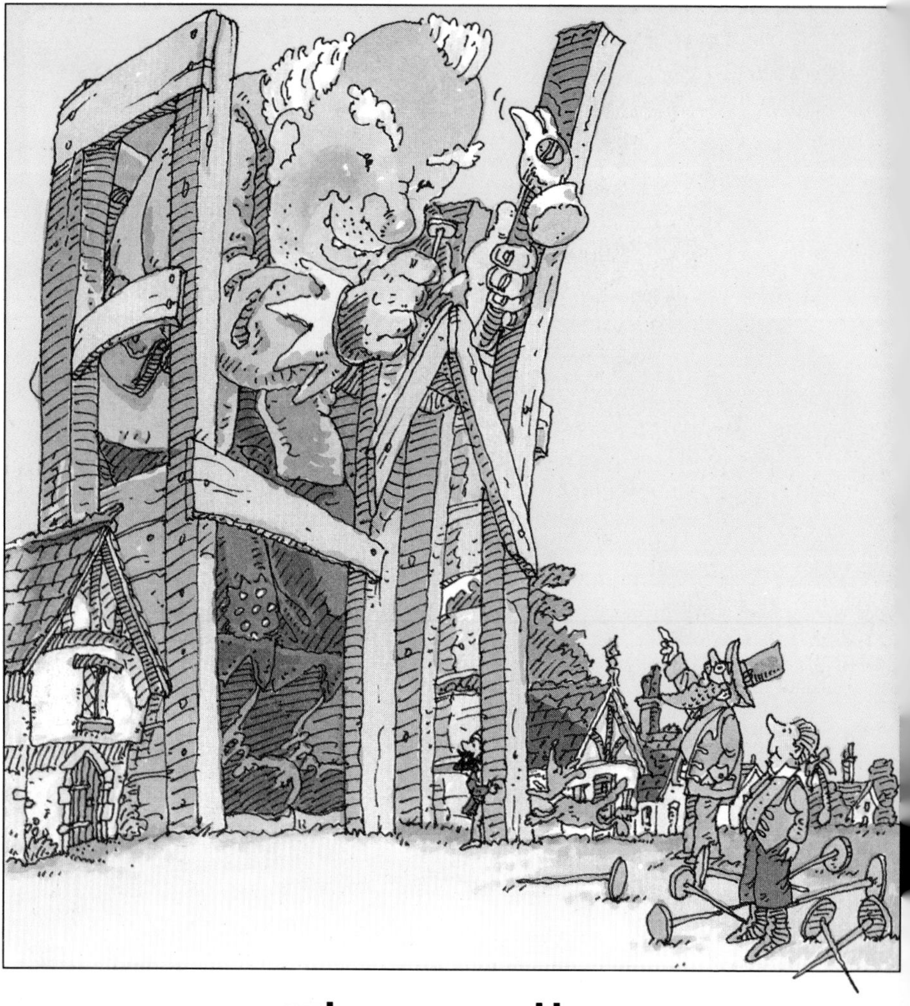

The walls.

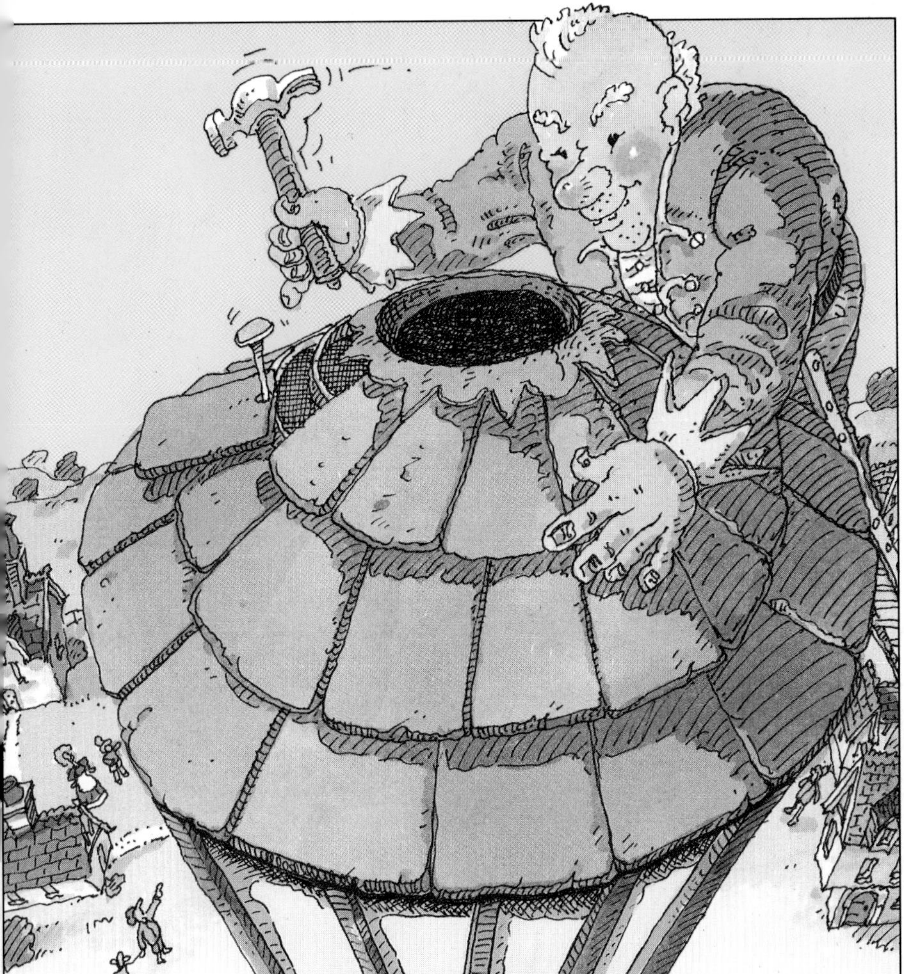

The roof.

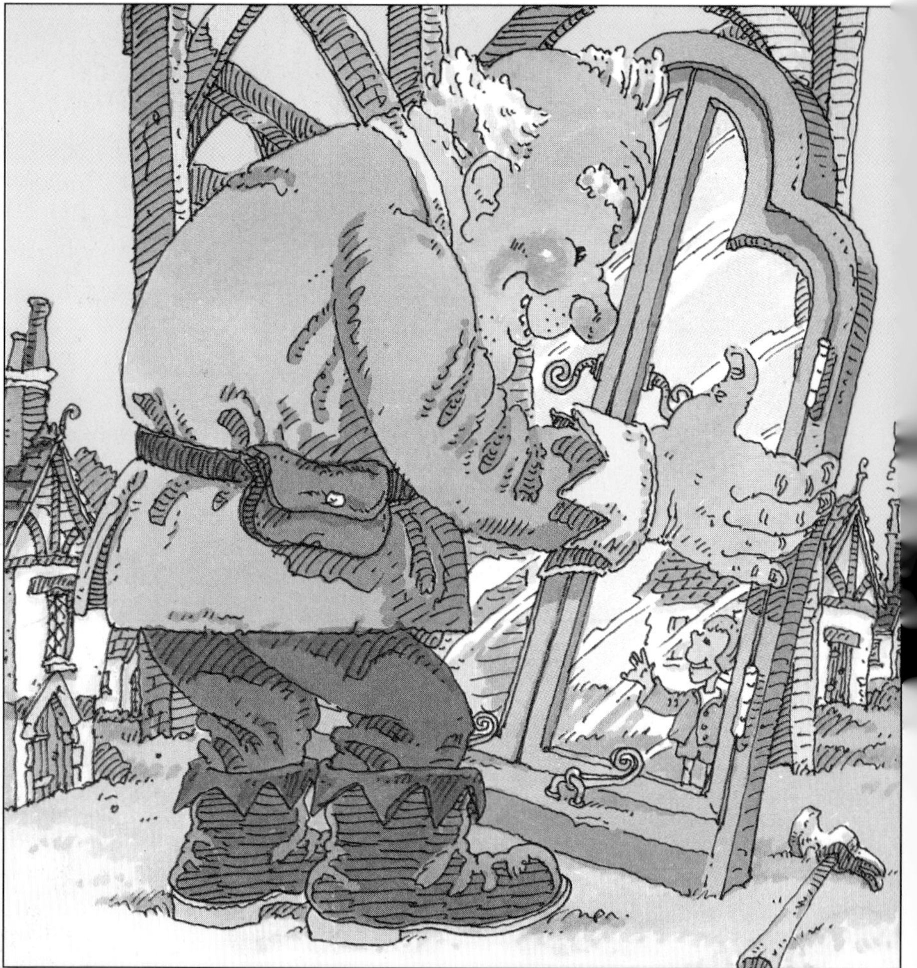

The windows.

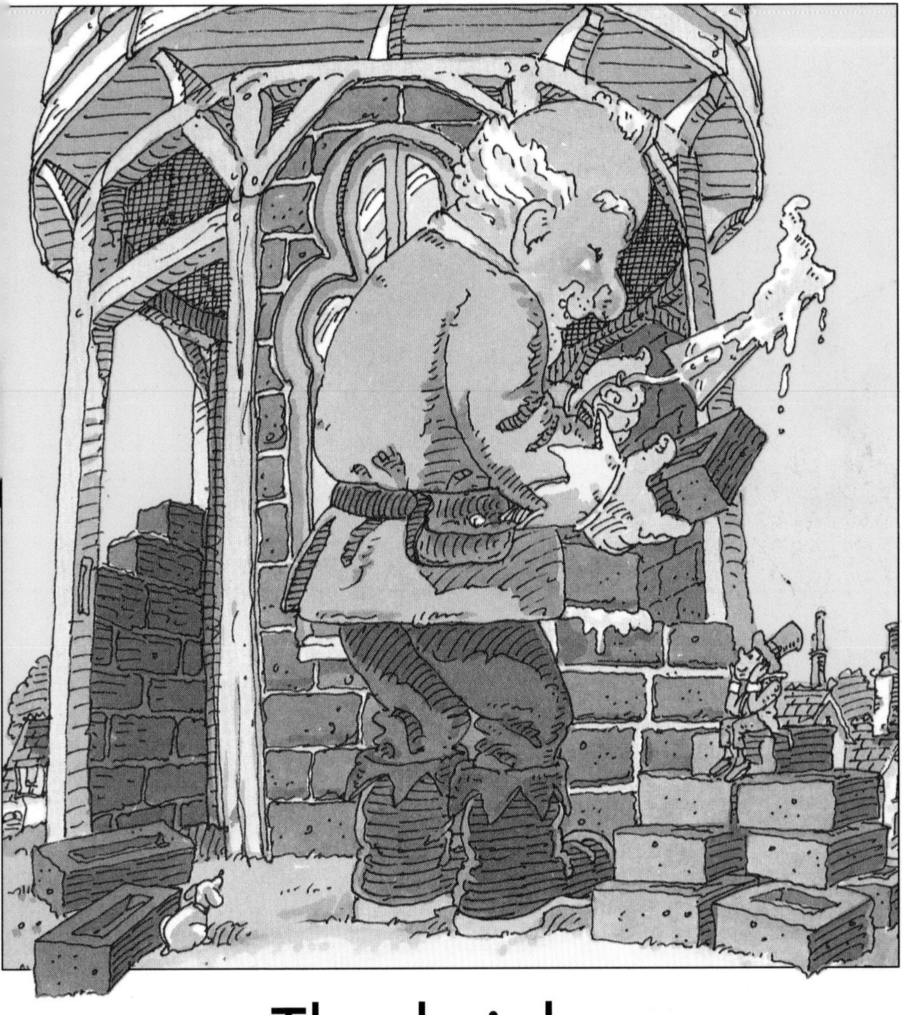

The bricks.

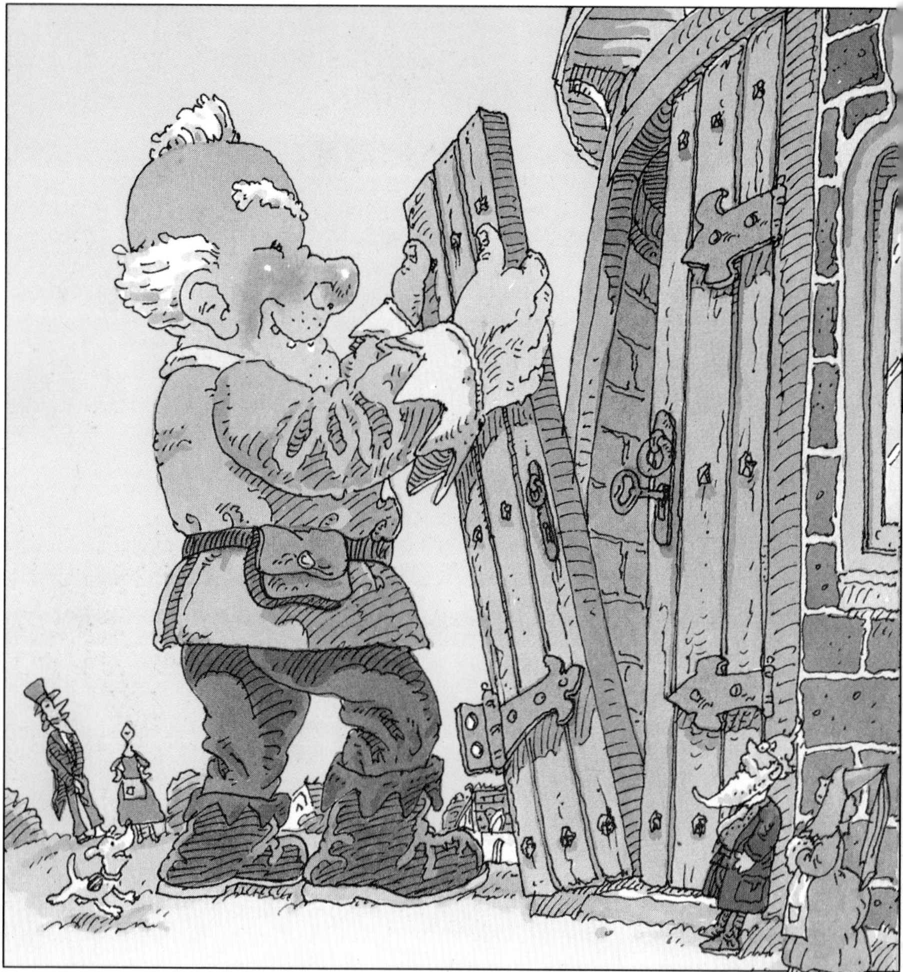

The doors.

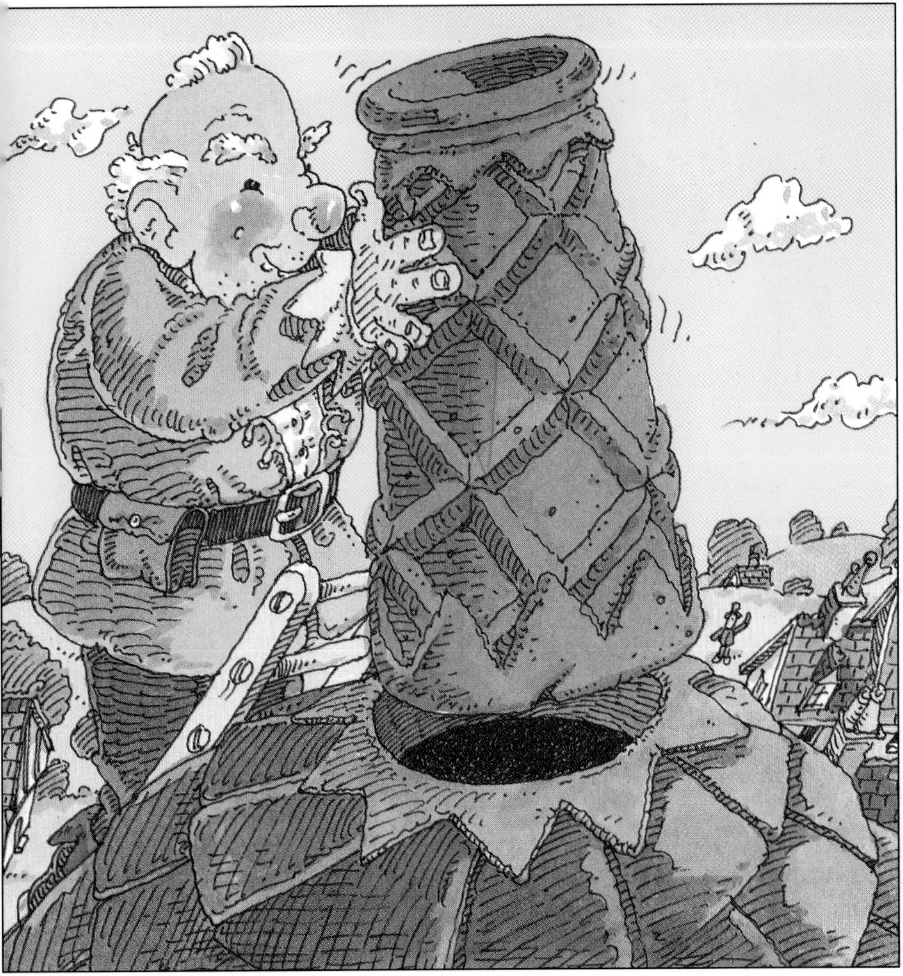

The chimney.

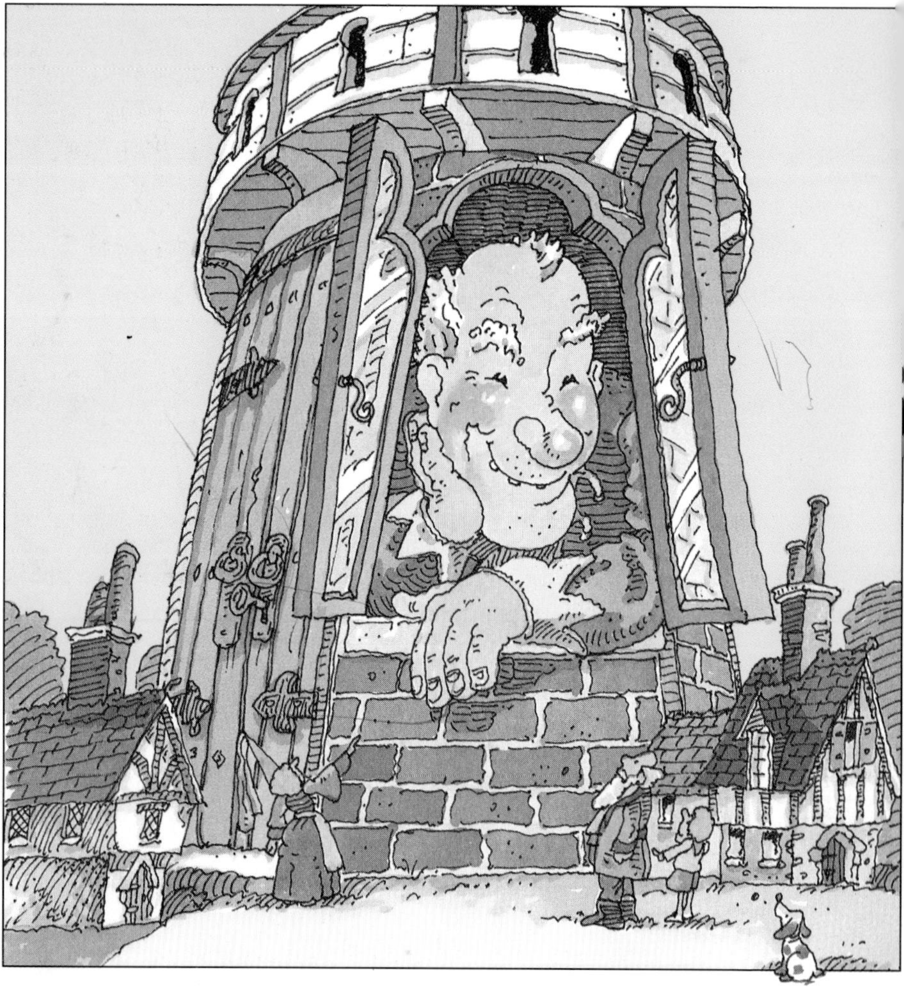

The new house.